THE LOTUS WITHIN

A Simple Guide to Inner Peace

Swamini Sri Lalitambika Devi

MAHAKAILASA ASHRAM

New York, New York

ISBN 978-0-9778633-8-9

TABLE OF CONTENTS

This handbook was written at the request of seekers in various psychiatric wards, drug rehabilitation centers, prisons, and homeless shelters.

You had wanted something to hold, so that you could continue meditating on your own. Please know that there is nothing to hold onto. Simply bring awareness to each thought, breath, word, and deed. Life and the true heart are the greatest teachers.

To meditate, just sit. Be gentle with your attention. Be regular in your efforts. Let love take care of everything else.

Here is a simple book that touches upon many of our discussions. It is an offering. If this may be useful to you, then I am glad.

——Swamini Sri Lalitambika Devi

Chapter I

CHILDHOOD

I learned to meditate when I was a child. My teacher was boyish and enthusiastic. He told of the infinite joy that is truly who we are. We rediscover ourselves through meditation.

He initiated me with a *mantra*, a secret word that holds the mystery of perfect fulfillment.

These *mantras* have been revealed to us by the ancient sages, and passed down from generation to generation. The mystical sound is repeated silently during the meditation sitting, until the mind subsides into boundless peace.

My teacher explained that the *mantra* was special. It was not to be revealed to anyone else, not even to my father who had arranged for me to learn to meditate.

The sacred *mantra* that this teacher transmitted was more a sound than a word. It could not be grasped with the mind. It floated free of image or association.

I remember sitting cross-legged, on a futon in my family's home by the ocean, with eyes closed, waiting.

To a child beginner, the practice initially felt static. Nothing seemed to be changing. I was sitting in the darkness behind my closed eyes and repeating the sound of the *mantra*. I was waiting for the magic to happen.

As new meditators, we are like children. We often hold the misconception that nothing is happening during our meditation or that we aren't meditating correctly. Sometimes, we leave the practice for a time, because we feel that we aren't getting results.

In fact, most of us don't know what we are seeking. We have no reference point for the meditative experience. We haven't yet sunk into the refuge of the heart, through which life becomes brand new, and love, limitless.

Until we experience the love that lives within, most of us spend our lives seeking happiness outside of ourselves. This is natural. To relieve our sense of longing, we strive to possess or achieve whatever we imagine will make us whole. Some of us believe we need the love of the right partner. Others seek prestige in our careers or a mammoth bank account. Still others turn from the path of family and career, in search of independence.

Somehow, once we get whatever we thought we needed to be happy, we find that something is still missing.

This creates confusion.

Ultimately, when we reach this point, we turn within to know the truth. This turn to the inside for fulfillment brings about our liberation from all sorrow.

❖ ❖ ❖

An old folk tale tells of this turn within. There once was a maiden who lived in a small cottage. The walls were built of wishing stone. Inside, there was only a rug woven from river grass, upon which she sat or slept. The birds carried food to her through a small, arched window, such that she was always well-nourished.

The maiden had experienced nothing beyond this tiny cottage, yet somehow, she felt that she was missing something. As the years passed, she wondered what it would be like to be free.

Each morning, she tried the wooden door to the cottage. It always seemed to be locked. No matter how hard she pushed against it, the door did not open. Though she called out in melodious tones, nobody came to her aid.

Each day, the sun rose and set in majestic glory. The stars glittered like jewels in the night sky, and again, soft dawn would break.

The seasons came and went. Autumn brought colorful leaves. Winter cloaked all with silence and snow. Spring scattered tender blossoms. Summer exuded fertile heat.

The earth continued to circle the sun, and the years passed.

The maiden sat and sat. Still, her mind was not quiet. She wanted something more.

One morning, as the maiden sat in the wishing cottage, a sudden inspiration struck her. She leapt up with grace and, once again, crossed the room to try the door.

Slowly, she turned the handle.

She let out a long breath.

The door opened. Suddenly, the maiden was free.

What had made the difference, after so many years?

Rather than pushing as hard as she could out against the door, the maiden had allowed the door to open inward.

Most of us live our lives as this maiden did, trying hard to free ourselves. In fact, we create our own resistance. We struggle with the world, and we fight against the mind.

When we become receptive, the door opens inward, easefully. We relax and receive. Grace and blessings abound.

In becoming vulnerable, we rediscover a love that knows no fear. It is a love of never having been hurt. It is a love of innocence—simple and boundless.

In opening inward, we discover infinite freedom. We rediscover the joy of who we have always been.

Chapter II

SUNLIGHT

Our true nature is like the sun. The sun depends on nothing outside of itself. It is self-illuminating. As such, it shines everywhere. It sheds light upon all beings without preference or limit, be they rock, dandelion, leopard, or child. What's more, the sun needs nothing in return.

Sufi poet Hafiz compares the soul to the sun. Hafiz lived in Persia during the 14th Century. He made his home in the garden city of Shiraz, where he became known as a beloved spiritual master. He shared of his ecstatic and mystical experiences through poems that are still enjoyed around the world today. In his poem "The Sun Never Says," he writes . . .

Even
after
all this time
the sun never says to the earth,

"You owe me."

Look
what happens
with a love like that—

it lights the whole
world.

Just as the sun shines, so the soul loves. True love is the nurturing parent. It is the attentive beloved. It is the amazed and reverent child. It is the friend in whom we confide everything. It is the benevolent and powerful master.

Such is our primordial nature. To radiate the light and warmth of unconditional love, like the sun, is an expression of the truth within.

Another well-loved reference to the sun appears in the Gayatri *mantra*. The Gayatri *mantra* is found in the *RgVeda*, one of four tomes said to be the most ancient Hindu scriptures. The *mantra* is named for its metre, which can be identified by three lines of eight syllables each.

Of course, we notice that this verse has four lines. The first line is an invocation.

The Gayatri *mantra* is said to be "the one that saves." It is the hero of sacred verse. These are words we may well look to when all seems to be lost. The lines express the radiance of pure consciousness.

Some make a meditation of chanting the verse with every breath. Others chant the verse 108 times in a sitting, as they rub each wooden bead of their *malas*. Still others awaken to chant it with the sunrise.

However we connect through the Gayatri *mantra,* the verse is an altruistic prayer for the awakening of all beings.

Om Bhur Bhuvah Svah
Tat Savitur Varenyam
Bhargo Devasya Dhimahi
Dhiyo Yo Nah Pracodayat

As noted, the actual *mantra* is preceded by an invocation. *Om Bhur Bhuvah Svah.* Salutations to the earth, the sky, and the heavens beyond.

This opening line can also be understood to salute the physical world of the senses, the subtle world of mind, and the *karmic* seed body from which these experiences are born. Such are the three states of conditioned existence.

The verse is well-loved, because it is rich with interpretation. Other states of three to which the opening invocation may refer include time, with its changing states of past, present, and future, as well as the cycle of creation, preservation, and reabsorption. The first line also alludes to the three states of consciousness—waking, dreaming, and deep sleep.

Illuminating all ephemeral experience is the light of awareness.

The Gayatri *mantra* compares this light of awareness to the brilliance of the sun. Like the sun's radiance, the light of liberated consciousness shines without external source. It is self-illuminating.

The verse is a universal prayer that all beings awaken to this divine light within. *Tat Savitur Varenyam, Bhargo Devasya Dhimahi, Dhiyo Yo Nah Pracodayat.* We meditate on that supreme and shining bliss. Like the sun, may that divine light within illuminate us all.

❖ ❖ ❖

The sun-like light of awareness is different from the light of a fire.

Firelight can be compared to the temporary happiness that we feel when we get something that we want. This might be anything from a slice of frosted layer cake, to a passionately adoring lover, to wealth, fame, and glory in our work life. Unfortunately, once we get what we thought would fulfill us, we find that we want something else. Such is our cyclic suffering.

Desire is the all-consuming fire. It constantly needs to be stoked.

Feeding the flames of desire brings about a bright and exciting blaze. Temporarily, we are relieved from the chill of our perceived isolation. Still, we are not free.

Our illusory sense of well-being depends upon re-kindling the fire for the warmth that we crave. We are endlessly fetching sticks and tinder in the form of stylish clothing, a sleek car, a spacious home, the right friends, the perfect partner, or a major promotion. There are no limits as to what we might desire.

This is the problem.

Just sit. Rest from all efforts to satisfy the hungry flames of desire.

With courage, we can turn to another source for comfort. As we give up grasping at ephemeral pleasures, we begin to bask in the warmth within. So, we awaken to true joy.

The warmth within depends on no external source. Because it is self-sustaining, it cannot be diminished. It is our primordial nature.

When we turn within, we realize that we have always been fulfilled. Like the sun, we shine with a light that is bright and steady. Our presence nourishes all. Truly, we are free.

May all beings awaken to this truth.

Chapter III

THE FULL MOON

As we awaken to inner fulfillment, we lose interest in the endless distraction of desire. We turn more and more of our attention to the truth within.

Truth is our first love. It is without cause and has neither beginning nor end. We are lost in the experience of it.

By losing ourselves in the love within, we become one with it. So, we realize that the pain of separation is nothing but a sweet and poignant illusion. We have always been complete. Forever have we been one with all.

The truth that illuminates our heart is in every being. We are surrounded by our own self in the form of all beings. Perhaps we feel the most immediate connection with family and friends. So too, we live as the breath of the grocer, the bank clerk, and the firefighter—people whose daily support we may take for granted. We are the expression in the eyes of all whom we pass on the street. We are the language of those whose words we cannot understand. Even the animals and the trees are our kin. So too, the earth, the rivers, and the sky are of our essence. To live in communion with all is to know that we are at once complete and of infinite potential.

This truth of oneness is expressed in verse through the *Upanishads*. The *Upanishads* reveal teachings of the awakened spiritual masters of India.

Upon realizing that worldly possessions and achievements could not bring happiness, the ancient sages retreated to the forest. There, amongst the birds and the trees, they lived a quiet life of inner reflection. As they realized the truth within, their presence became so powerful as to draw true seekers to them. Those who were lucky enough to sit at their feet wrote down their words for posterity.

No one knows exactly when the teachings were written down. We can guess that they were scribed about five hundred years before the birth of Jesus Christ.

The wisdom is timeless.

The poetry is a map to the heart. It lays the foundation for self-realization and absolute freedom.

These verses express truth that is beyond sacred ritual and the learned mind. The words of the great sages come from a direct experience with pure consciousness. Such is the light of infinite inner perfection that shines forth from the cave of the heart.

❖ ❖ ❖

The *Isha Upanishad* opens with a peace *mantra*. Isha is like a pet-name for the personal God, who would otherwise be referred to as Ishvara. The name Isha also comes from the verb root *ish*, meaning to rule. We can think of these words as close, personal instruction from a wise and loving parent, friend, beloved, or master.

Purnamadah Purnamidam
Purnat Purnamudachyate
Purnasya Purnamadaya
Purnamevavasisyate

Repeated throughout the verse is the word *purnam*. *Purnam* means fullness, wholeness, completion, or perfection. It means lacking nothing. Such is our basic nature.

We may not immediately recognize our inherent goodness. Instead, we live with the unspoken sense that something is missing. What it is, we can't be sure. Those around us appear to be happy, which only leaves us feeling out of place. So, we live in desperate search of that which we do not know.

This gaping sense of need is, however, an illusion.

Think of the moon. The moon goes through phases, or so it seems. On some nights, it glows as a half-moon. On other nights, the moon appears to be no more than a sliver of light. When the moon is completely illuminated by the sun's rays, it shows itself to be full.

Similar to the word *purnam*, the word *purnima* means "full moon."

Really, the moon does not change shape or size. When the sun's light shines directly upon it, we see the moon for what it is. Through the darkest of nights, when it does not even appear to shine, the moon has always been full.

So it is with the heart. As we awaken to the inner light of consciousness, we realize that we have always been fulfilled. We are now and ever have been perfect, just as we are.

Purnamadah Purnamidam. All arises from the source that is neither perfect or imperfect but absolute in all.

The circumstances of our lives are an expression of pure consciousness that seeks to awaken unto itself. Transcendent perfection brings forth a world that is perfect in its apparent imperfection.

We realize that all is right within and with the world by expressing gratitude. We begin to appreciate the blessings, rather than focusing on the difficulties. So, we find a renewed strength to accept what is. In this way, we are able to learn from the world of ephemeral creation.

Through our daily interactions, we receive the teachings needed to realize our innate perfection.

Life is a playground through which we rediscover our divine nature and return to the source. We need not take ourselves or our circumstances quite so seriously.

As we open to the lighter side of life, we awaken to truth. Suddenly, I am you, and you are me.

The particular circumstances of our lives are perfect for us to realize who we really are. Pure consciousness supports us in our yearnings, our wanderings, and finally, in our realization of ourselves as that source of all being.

❖ ❖ ❖

Purnat Purnamudacyate. What is complete arises from what is complete. Even so, all remains complete.

Think of the birth of a child. The mother brings forth a complete being with unlimited potential from her womb. Still, she loses nothing of herself. She remains whole. So, as consciousness brings forth world after world, that transcendent and primordial bliss remains complete.

Indian mythology is rife with stories of creation. The Divine Mother creates and recreates the world with the blink of her eyes. So say the goddesses of speech in the thousand-line hymn *Sri Lalita Sahasranama*.

In the *Chandogya Upanishad,* the sage Uddalaka teaches his son Shvetaketu a different tale of creation: Existence brings forth the cosmos of itself and then enters into everything.

"You are that!" Uddalaka tells his son, speaking of the truth in all.

Whether we identify with a divine being or formless truth, the point is that we are all an expression of created perfection.

Purnasya Purnamadaya Purnamevavasisyate. As consciousness reabsorbs its creation, all remains complete.

Just as the ocean absorbs rivers and rain without overflowing, so the source of all being reabsorbs its creation without change.

From a personal perspective, this also means that we can handle loss. When a loved one dies, we remain whole. What we call "death" is actually the continuation of the soul's journey, or perhaps it is final liberation—reabsorption into the source.

We feel grief when we lose someone, but we need not be derailed by it. We allow the feelings to arise and subside, like waves on the ocean.

We are gentle with ourselves during this time of loss and healing. Even so, we continue.

In understanding the fragility of life, we express our love fully to those around us. We don't wait until someone is on the deathbed to say *Thank you for being in my life* or *I love you*.

Mired in the sorrow of loss, we renew ourselves at the fountain of appreciation. In the midst of grieving, we can imagine what life would have been like without our loved one. We rediscover joy in being thankful for having known this sacred being.

Throughout our life's journey, we may experience small "deaths." Perhaps we lose a job, a friend, or some sum of money. We might even lose our health, our mind, or our external freedom for a period of time.

Whenever the ground shakes like this, we are being offered a sacred and particular teaching. Loss is a pointer to that which never dies. It is an awakening to who we are beyond this body and this mind. It is the call of spirit.

Tapping our inner strength, we continue on the journey. Rather than resisting, we allow transformation to take place. As we open to each perfect teaching, so we awaken.

Chapter IV

THE LOTUS WITHIN

When I first arrived in India, I was amazed by the illuminating presence of the *guru*. It seemed that when the awakened one walked, be it past the *puja* temple with its fragrant fire or into a conference room full of government officials, there was something within that wasn't moving at all.

One of the monks explained, "You become a *swami*, when you know that everything you need is within you."

I admired the quiet dignity of the monks. Compassion and devotion were expressed in their every action.

I tried to sink into that inner stillness when I meditated, and as I did my *seva* around the *ashram*.

Wherever we find ourselves, we awaken through the *guru's* grace. We are always in the presence of the *guru*, for the true *guru* lives within.

The *Chandogya Upanishad* calls this space within "the lotus of the heart." The *Upanishad* says that as vast as the infinite space beyond is the space within, the lotus of the heart. Knowing this, all desires are fulfilled.

To consider such an idea is mind-blowing.

It's supposed to be. Only when we let go of the thinking mind can we experience truth. As the mind aligns with spirit, thinking is completely absorbed. So, experience becomes direct.

The lotus of the heart is the infinite space of such realizations.

In India, the lotus in full bloom is a symbol of liberation. The lotus grows up from the mud at the bottom of a river. The muddy river bottom nourishes the budding flower. Once it blooms, the lotus is such that it cannot be disturbed. The flower floats in the middle of the river, yet is untouched by the waters.

It turns its face to the sun.

Lotus petals are the stuff of legend, for anything that falls onto the bloom rolls right off of it. The flower remains ever radiant and pure.

Our hearts are like the lotus flower. The journey to realization can be compared to an inner blossoming. The opening of the heart is nourished by what we might consider to be the mud, or perhaps the mulch, in our lives.

Through life's challenges, we get to know our patterned emotional responses. We grow up from the mud, so to speak. If we have the courage to acknowledge with tender compassion when and how we feel stuck in the mud, we can be free. It is not in denying the mud but in making use of it that we blossom.

The open lotus is a symbol for the *jivanmukta*, one who lives liberated in the world. Such a one, in full bloom, spreads the fragrance of boundless joy.

Sun Bu-er is one of the most beloved teachers of Taoism. She lived in China during the 12th Century. After raising three children, she became a nun. Said to have reached complete realization, as did her husband, she is known through folklore as one of the Seven Immortals.

She writes of the lotus . . .

Cut brambles long enough,
Sprout after sprout,

And the lotus will bloom
Of its own accord:
Already waiting in the clearing,
The single image of light.
The day you see this,
That day you will become it.

With calm awareness, we prune the brambles of the mind. These brambles are the thoughts and emotions upon which we get snagged. They are the thorns of our desires and demands, our prickly insistence on having things go our way. They are the voice of self-doubt and inner criticism.

We prune gently. We recognize these disturbances of mind with compassion for ourselves and for those around us.

Even as we make our best efforts, we remain receptive to grace. Remember, the lotus is already waiting in the clearing.

When we relax the mind, the inner light becomes apparent. So, we become that light.

As the lotus of the heart blooms, we open to our most natural way of being. We find the space to be who we are. We begin to live a life that is meaningful. We feel connection with all being. We are the bright and steady radiance of unconditioned love.

Chapter V

FIVE VEILS

Five illusions of personal identity veil who we truly are. Though they may be attractive, the veils delude us into thinking that we are something we are not.

The sage of the *Taittiriya Upanishad* names the five veils as body, energy, mind, wisdom, and bliss.

These are referred to as the *annamaya kosha*, the *pranamaya kosha*, the *manomaya kosha*, the *vijnanamaya kosha*, and the *anandamaya kosha*. They can be imagined as a set of Russian dolls—one within another, within another . . .

In any language, land, or era, these five experiences are relative.

Still, we mistake ourselves for one or more of the five *koshas*.

We may feel an attachment to them, because we like them. Perhaps we appreciate the way we look, trounce others with our intellect, or bask in the warmth of inner bliss.

We may also insist upon the *koshas* because we don't know anything beyond them. We defend their reality, for we are afraid that we would be nothing without them.

These five are named as veils, however, because they can be parted.

In the *Mundaka Upanishad*, the sage Angiras tells his disciple of two kinds of knowledge— the higher and the lower.

The higher, *paravidya*, is the clear light of unconditioned being. This truth is innate.

The lower, *aparavidya*, is learned through the mind. It is knowledge of the created world, including such things as astronomy, medicine, music, literature, religion, and even our sense of self.

Angiras compares the created world to the gossamer web that the spider spins and then withdraws back unto itself. This is the cosmic web through which the creator moves freely.

Like the spider, we create the personal web in which we live. Our web is the projection of these illusions of self, the five *koshas*. We, however, are bound by our web.

Understand that we need not negate the experience of body, vigor, emotion, wisdom, or bliss to be free. Rather, we seek to understand them, so that we can awaken to a greater truth.

In appreciating the five *koshas*, we draw them back into ourselves. We realize our identity with the source of this creation. So, we are liberated.

Annamaya Kosha

The first of the five *koshas* is the physical body. This outermost sheath is the most obvious veil. It often gives the first impression of who we are.

Even so, the body is ever-changing. Someone who has not seen us since childhood might not recognize us as a maturing adult, or as a wise elder.

The body is constantly transforming. Science has shown that the skin renews itself every seven days, that the blood cells change over every ninety days, and that the entire body is made new every seven years.

This is good news. There is room for growth, healing, and transformation.

It also makes clear that we don't look to our body as a definitive identity.

The body is simply a vehicle in which we pursue our dreams, including that of absolute freedom. It's like the car in which we ride to reach our destination.

On a road trip, we keep our car well-fueled and tuned up.

Similarly, we keep the body in good condition for this life's journey. We fuel the body with a light and balanced diet. We tune the body through regular exercise. We take care to keep the body clean and clear of toxins.

We don't focus on the body as an end in itself. We do keep it healthy and strong, so that we can continue on the road to realization without the distraction of injury or illness.

❖ ❖ ❖

Even as we do our best to maintain health and strength, we each have the potential to experience pain and illness. Such is the vulnerability of the physical body.

It's important to realize that a breakdown is not the end of the world, or of our world.

Though initially distracting, pain or illness can be a doorway to spiritual realization. Difficult experiences offer the potential for transformation.

Each situation in our life occurs because we have something to learn. Instead of asking why something has happened, we can open to the situation. We take an interest in the opportunity to expand our consciousness. Once the lesson is learned, the situation resolves itself.

Understand that a teaching may be received through the physical body, though the actual evolution that takes place is spiritual.

The key element to positive transformation is connection. The power of the resulting spiritual experience depends upon how we relate to the physical, and the related emotional, experience.

Any kind of suffering is a signpost to turn within. When we realize the impermanence of the material world, we turn within to seek a deeper truth. So, we awaken to an unshakeable inner peace.

❖ ❖ ❖

We might imagine that if the pain of illness or injury can be a doorway to realization, then so could physical pleasure. This may be a seductive idea, but such a path is risky. Here's why. The experience of pain is not something that we wish to extend. On the other hand, we might like to remain in a pleasurable state for as long as possible, and then to repeat the experience endlessly.

Laboratory mice who are offered a free-flowing supply of cocaine will continue to partake of it, forgoing food and sleep, until they die of exhaustion. They don't understand what the long-term outcome of their choices will be.

Such an experiment seems unnecessarily cruel. It proves nothing that we do not already know. More of a pleasurable experience isn't necessarily better.

Often, however, we act like caged, addicted mice. We want more of whatever seems like a good thing—sex, money, or power.

If you were king or queen for a day, would you seek endless pleasure or the liberation of all beings? Contemplate this question deeply. It touches upon the source of primordial truth.

❖ ❖ ❖

The intermittence of pleasure and pain are as natural as the fluctuating tides of the ocean. High tide is balanced by low tide. We cannot hold onto either. When we experience one, we can expect the other to follow.

So it is with partners like loss and gain, praise and blame, or infamy and fame. If we seek one, we are welcoming the other.

One who is serious about liberation is not interested in these experiences of worldly duality. The true seeker is not a pleasure-seeker.

Remember Pinocchio and his buddies on Pleasure Island. At first, the days of endless goodies and fun seem like a bountiful vacation. Soon, however, those who cared only for pleasing themselves turned into donkeys and were sent to work in the bitter salt mines.

We are each living out the quest to be real, with no strings attached.

When we get real, we are genuinely unselfish. The liberated being wants nothing but the joyous liberation of all beings.

This is the purpose of our birth. The body is not a means for us to be ensnared by pleasure. It is an instrument to realize truth, to be liberated, and to live in joyous service to all.

Pranamaya Kosha

The *pranamaya kosha* is often called the breath body, or the vital body. Breath is the expression of our vitality. We call this vitality *prana*.

In the *Prasna Upanishad*, six seekers approach the sage Pippalada to ask about the truth of existence.

To the sincere Kausalya, Pippalada explains that *prana* is like the chief of the body, with its sense organs and functions. *Prana* enlivens the eye, the ear, the nose, and the tongue. *Prana* enlivens speech, the hands and the feet, and the organs of excretion and procreation.

Prana, too, is that by which the breath breathes.

In the subtle realm, *prana* is like a wind that wafts through the mind. The movement of *prana* causes thoughts to arise. The nature of our thoughts depends upon which way the wind blows, so to speak.

Our past thoughts, words, and deeds create *samskaras*, or impressions in the mind. As the winds of *prana* blow, it is natural that they flow through these created channels. This is why we have thinking patterns.

With awareness, we can transform our thinking patterns. When we work with *prana*, we are not only energizing the body but also calming the mind.

The simplest way to work with *prana* is to notice the breath.

Ultimately, our gentle attention to the breath liberates the life force, heals the troubled mind, and leads to full awakening.

Manomaya Kosha

The *manomaya kosha* is the sheath of mind. Where exactly does mind reside? We cannot point to it. The mind, however, directs the energy and activities of the entire physical body.

On an emotional level, the mind keeps us under the illusion that we are separate from other beings. It maintains the ideology of yours and mine, as well as attraction and aversion.

Without knowing better, we identify with the *manomaya kosha*. We believe that the way we experience the world is the way the world really is, for everyone throughout time and space.

We fail to understand that what we are experiencing is a direct result of our own thoughts, words, and deeds. The world as it appears to us is a reflection of how we live our life. Therefore, if we wish to be happy, it is best to live kindly.

The mind is also a veil through which we understand ourselves. Most of us are mistaken about who we are. We think, *I am an angry person*. We think, *I am fearful*. We think, *I am not able to change*. We believe in our ideas and feelings as a dogmatic creed by which our actions are determined. We mistake conditioned personality for our natural state of being.

Our sense of self, however, is limited by what we learn. We take in what other people tell us about who we are. Then, we react to these ideas. We may accept and magnify them. We may also rebel against them. So, our self-image continues to evolve.

What we think of ourselves is like a wall we build. It's protective. It may be strong and attractive. Still, it keeps us from truly knowing ourselves and others. With great courage, we can dismantle the wall, brick by brick.

We continue to learn through experience. With attention and kindness, we can repattern our thinking and our behavior. We can live at ease with ourselves and the world around us.

❖ ❖ ❖

It's important to acknowledge that there is value to the emotional mind. Emotion is a means of communication. It lets other people know how we are feeling. An emotional response, like a smile, may communicate more immediately and sincerely than words.

Emotion can also be a guide. Fear, for example, lets us know when we are in danger and need to protect ourselves. A feeling of well-being, on the other hand, may signal that we are on the right track with what we are doing.

Emotion even has the potential to create confusion. Imbalanced emotion distorts our experience of self and the world around us. These misunderstandings, however, are a doorway through which can we realize truth.

In appreciating the emotions that capture our attention, we realize that they are, like the view seen through a kaleidoscope, ever-transforming. As such, they are not the truth of who we are.

We don't reject emotion. We turn towards it. We open around our feelings to discover the greater space of awareness.

Neti Neti is a Vedic injunction.

Not this. Not this.

In attending to and releasing from the mind what is not truth, we realize what really matters.

We wise up. We mature. We learn to get along in the world, so that we can continue smoothly on the journey.

We discover a sense of trust in the big picture of how things are working. We are motivated by an unshakeable confidence that we will know the true love within. Freedom is not only for those who are far off in some mystical land. It is for us, just as we are in this moment.

Vijnanamaya Kosha

Behind the veil of mind flutters the veil of wisdom. Wisdom purifies the emotional mind. Wisdom allows us to be comfortably poised, rather than flamboyantly dramatic or rigidly logical. With compassion and understanding, wisdom takes an interest in the changing experiences of the emotional mind.

The veil of wisdom can be compared to what Sigmund Freud calls the super-ego.

Freud was a nineteenth-century Austrian neurologist who introduced the world to psychoanalysis. Through dialogue between patient and analyst, psychoanalysis treats psychopathology by bringing repressed memories from the unconscious mind to the light of the conscious mind, thereby freeing the patient of their latent influence.

Freud posited a model of the mind as being constructed from the id, or our often-repressed primal desires, the ego, or the organizing principle that seeks to satisfy the id's desires, and the super-ego, or that which exercises morality and helps us to get along in the world.

Freud once said, "He does not believe that does not live according to his belief."

Deep down, we know the right thing to do. The veil of wisdom, or the super-ego, is like our conscience.

We can trust ourselves. We can be brave enough to let go of desire, anger, and fear for the sake of freedom. We can live in harmony with our deepest truth.

Scholar, doctor, and mystic, the Indian sage Patanjali also examines the nature of the mind. Said to have been born when the world was created, Patanjali scribed the *Yoga Sutras*. These 196 aphorisms are the foundation of *Yoga* philosophy. Here, Patanjali offers an eight-limbed system as a means to free the mind of its neuroses and hang-ups.

Pataanjali suggests *svadhyaya,* or self-study, as a means to freedom. He names self-study, along with purity, contentment, discipline, and surrender, as five virtues to be cultivated.

Svadhyaya can be understood in two ways.

On a personal level, we study our psychology. We look into the mind and its reactions. We get to know our mental obstacles and illusions, so that we can be free of them.

On a universal level, we study the ways of the liberated spiritual masters—their poetry, their philosophy, their lives, and their silence. We immerse ourselves in ideas of absolute truth.

So, wisdom awakens.

We are then able to respond effectively to the challenges that we face. Rather than acting impulsively, we calmly consider all sides of a situation. We allow our response to arise from the wise heart.

When wisdom awakens, we may even choose to pursue a path that will lead us safely through the unhappy snares of the material world to the boundless joy of liberation.

Anandamaya Kosha

The innermost veil is one of bliss.

True liberation means knowing ourselves beyond even this veil of personal bliss.

Wow, I feel good again. Finally, I am free, we might say.

The sages tell us otherwise.

Zen Master Kakuan, who lived in China during the 12th Century, gives us the *Oxherding Tale*. Told through drawings and verse, the teaching illuminates the desire for inner bliss as something to leave behind, if we are to progress towards full enlightenment.

The tale opens with the seeker searching for the ox. The ox has never really gone astray, but the seeker is confused and so searches for it. *The ox is our true nature.*

The seeker is lost. She wanders through forest and mountain, until she comes upon the ox's hoofprints. *The path is discovered.*

Suddenly, the seeker catches her first glimpse of the ox. *Whatever this first experience is, it points to the source of all being.*

The seeker grasps hold of the rope, catches the ox, and struggles as the ox charges up the mountain. *The seeker turns from the material world. She stays connected, as she begins to tame the mind.*

The mind may be stubborn and unpredictable. Here begins sincere meditation practice.

The seeker tends to the ox, gently taming it, until it willingly follows. *The seeker has turned within. Now, mental elaboration is recognized as self-created delusion. Inner peace arises.*

The seeker rides the ox down from the mountain and back to her village. *Upon realization, the seeker need not remain in solitude. She returns to ordinary, daily life.*

The ox disappears. *The sense of duality vanishes. To live in the mountains or the village makes no difference. Between the mundane and the sacred, there is no difference. As to the individual and the whole, there is no difference. There is no difference.*

Understand that this tale may be interpreted in different ways. The point here is that, upon taming the ox, the seeker returns to the village. We give up the idea that we need to separate ourselves from ordinary, daily life to live as a liberated being. We participate as usual, with a new awareness.

The liberated ones are joyful. They offer themselves for the benefit of all beings.

The ever-free reflect our potential. They are none other than our true self that has realized its union with all being and the source of creation.

❖ ❖ ❖

Once we understand the five *koshas*, we may experience them all simultaneously, even as we identify with none of them.

We also realize the union of created being; we are all interconnected.

In fact, we can think of each *kosha* as being not only individual but also collective. This body of flesh, bone, soft tissue, and fluids is composed of the same elements as every body, as well as the rivers, trees, stars, and the midnight sky. The physical body is as fragrant and delicious as ripe fruit, as loveable as a kitten, and as precious as a diamond.

The subtle body is that of breath, mind, and wisdom. It is one of inner experience.

This subtle body, too, is simultaneously individual and collective. Realize that the breath in one is the same as the breath in all beings. Similarly, if we understand our mind, then we know all mind. Meanwhile, the seed of wisdom waits to sprout in each of our hearts.

So too, the state of bliss is one in all.

The bliss body is also known as the soul. Through soul awareness, we heal from the illusion of pain and separation. It is the soul that rises with yearning at the call of the source. It is the soul that loses itself in the source, as a river flows and disappears into the ocean.

As we part the five *koshas*, we realize absolute union. This is a liberated existence that transcends body, breath, mind, wisdom, and even personal bliss.

When we realize the light of the true self, we have also caught a glimpse of the benevolent source of all being. In letting go of ourselves as this individual and merging with that primordial source, we awaken to absolute freedom.

Chapter VI

THE TREE OF CONSCIOUSNESS

Little is known of the sage Kapila but his teachings. Kapila is the founder of *Samkhya*, one of the six classical Indian philosophies. The school of *Samkhya* explains our awakening through the image of a tree. This is the tree of consciousness.

As are the five *koshas*, the tree of consciousness is a way of understanding our constructed identity, so that we can be free of this limitation.

The tree of consciousness rises from sensory experience, through mind, ego, wisdom, and sacred duality, and finally reaches the light of truth.

In simple form, the tree is rooted in the sense experiences of the physical body—sight, sound, scent, taste, and touch.

Physical sensation is then identified by the mind, or *manas*. For example, "This taste on my tongue is ripe mango."

After the mind identifies a sensation, the ego, *ahamkara*, comments on the experience.

The ego is the seat of individual preference.

The ego likes or dislikes that which is identified by mind. For example, "I like the taste of this mango, and I want more of it."

The ego might also notice that there is a better mango to be had, perhaps someone else's mango. We imagine that what someone else has is sweeter than the fruit in our hand.

Sometimes, the frustrated ego even says, "I can't stand this kind of fruit, and I must have no more of it."

The ego is sure that happiness depends upon the duality of attraction and aversion.

The ego is also concerned with the idea of I, me, and mine. It is a trapped sense of self. It attaches us to the world, engaging us in a never-ending bid to have things go our way.

Seated above the ego is wisdom, or *buddhi*. Wisdom recognizes the desires of the ego from a place of clarity. Wisdom understands that the ego's needs change from moment to moment. As such, these desires can never be satisfied. Spending our time trying to fulfill the wishes of the capricious ego is like trying to fill a broken bucket. The water will always leak from the bottom. The task cannot be completed. Try as we might, we will never fulfill the ego from a place of ego.

Wisdom recognizes the futility of trying to satisfy the ego's desires. Consciousness rises.

As consciousness rises, we see more clearly what will bring lasting joy. We lose concern for the ego's demands. We turn from empty distraction. We seek not the pleasurable but the good.

In the *Katha Upanishad*, Yama, the Lord of Death, teaches the young boy Nachiketa the secrets of immortality. One of his first instructions is to seek not the pleasant but the good. We renounce *preya* for *sreya*.

This doesn't mean that we purposefully incur suffering for ourselves. In giving up the pleasant for the good, we are not denying ourselves anything worthwhile.

Yama urges us to recognize that indulging in short-term pleasure does not bring about lasting benefit. It may even be detrimental to our health, state of mind, or spiritual awakening.

In contrast, what is good may not seem to be immediately desirable, however, embracing the good will ultimately liberate us.

In the *Bhagavad Gita*, Sri Krishna, charioteer to the despondent warrior Arjuna, offers similar advice. When explaining the different kinds of happiness, Sri Krishna points out that what tastes sweet going down may be digested as poison, whereas a bitter medicine may bring about healing and strength.

To understand the difference between the pleasurable and the good is the awakening of wisdom. Now, our choices arise from clarity, rather than passion.

Soon, the tree branches out. Here, we experience a spiritualized sense of duality. We distinguish the mundane from the sacred, or that which is created from that which is pure spirit.

Samkhya calls these dimensions *prakrti* and *purusa*. *Prakrti* includes the body-mind, as well as the world around us. *Purusa* is the light within.

When we first taste of *purusa*, we may be filled with a desire to turn from the world and do nothing but enjoy this experience. We feel the tender yearning for lasting fulfillment. This longing leads us to merge with all that is, will be, and ever has been.

As consciousness continues to rise, our self-consciousness disappears. The world around us disappears, and we disappear, too. The individual soul disappears into the source of all being.

We awaken to recognize the self in every being. Meditative absorption is sacred. So too is the created world a sacred emanation of the source.

We have transcended duality, altogether.

We are in all, and all is in us.

Chapter VII

AN INDIAN FIG TREE

The Indian fig tree, also known as the banyan tree, can be recognized by its roots. The roots are aerial, growing upward. Meanwhile, the tree's branches drop down towards the earth.

In the *Bhagavad Gita*, Sri Krishna tells his disciple Arjuna of this unusual tree. The *asvattha* tree is rooted in worldly action, even as the leaves of this fabled tree are the sacred pages of the *Vedas*. The *asvattha* tree is unconventional. It is does not comply with expectation. It is, in fact, upside down.

The word *asvattha* refers to the instability of material and emotional experience. It means that which is different today from what it was yesterday.

Of course, when we want to keep things as they are, change brings suffering. We cannot find lasting happiness in the ever-shifting illusion of worldly experience.

Sri Krishna explains that the seeker need only cut the tree of illusion at its roots to be free of all sorrow.

The tree can be felled with the axe of wisdom. Wisdom sees through superficial worldly attraction. When we cut through the craving for material things that can't bring lasting satisfaction, we open to spiritual bliss.

❖ ❖ ❖

Three qualities keep us rooted to the material world and its sorrows.

These qualities of nature are known as the *gunas*. They are *tamas*, *rajas*, and *sattva*. The three are explained as darkness, desire, and light. They can also be experienced as lethargy, passion, and clarity. They may even be felt as inertia, activity, and balance.

The three *gunas* are qualities of personality. We can understand ourselves and our moods by noticing which of the *gunas* is predominant in our mind at a given time.

When darkness, heaviness, or lethargy gets the better of us, we may feel unmotivated or even depressed.

As passion takes over, we are motivated to work hard and to achieve. The catch is that we are energized by personal desire. So, we become ensnared in the cycle of "never enough."

With greater clarity, we ease up on striving for personal gain. Still, we want to be good. Perhaps we are trying to relieve our suffering, impress a teacher, or build a happier future for ourselves and others.

There is nothing wrong with wanting to be good. We simply recognize that this is not yet the fully awakened experience. Doing good deeds is the final stepping stone to liberation.

The secret to working successfully with the *gunas* is that each quality of illusion overcomes another. When we are stuck in the sloth of *tamas*, passionate desire will motivate us to make change. Passion's selfish and insatiable hunger is then relieved by the wish to be good. Still, we are not liberated. *Sattvoguna* is like a chain of pure gold. Although it is attractive and expresses a wealth of virtue, it is still a form of bondage.

Sri Ramakrishna, a nineteenth-century Bengali saint, describes the *gunas* as three robbers. These three robbers surround a young man who has lost his way in the woods. *Tamas*, the dark thief, wants to kill him and steal his wealth. *Rajas*, filled with binding desire, suggests that they tie the man to a tree and then steal his wealth. *Sattva* pacifies *tamas* and *rajas*, takes the man's hand, and shows him the path home.

As attractive as *sattva* seems, we must even let go of goodness and of the path itself, if we are to be truly free.

❖ ❖ ❖

Lao Tzu, a Taoist philosopher whose name means "Old Master," offers words of wisdom on giving up goodness. Lao Tzu lived in China, where he was a contemporary of Confucius. He also lived around the same time that the sages of the *Upanishads* were teaching in the forests of India.

Lao Tzu, too, retreated from society. Meanwhile, he wrote on the benevolent potential of government, work, and family life, as guidance to the individual who wishes to feel whole again. This classic treatise is known as the *Tao te Ching*.

The first verses explain that all arises from unity.

In naming one quality, however, we bring its opposite into existence. When we see some people or experiences as good, others become bad.

To remedy this self-created duality, Lao Tzu suggests that we give up personal intention. This includes the intent to be good.

Lao Tzu posits *wu wei*, or non-doing. We don't refuse to participate with the world, but we do so without seeking a particular outcome for ourselves. We allow truth to manifest through us. In this way, what we do arises from the whole and is of benefit to all. We rediscover the source of all being.

Rumi, a thirteenth-century Persian mystic, also writes on transcending the dualities of the world. Rumi was a Sufi who expressed his ecstasy in verse. . . .

> *Out beyond ideas of wrongdoing*
> *and rightdoing,*
> *there is a field. I'll meet you there.*
> *When the soul lies down*
> *in that grass,*

the world is too full to talk about.
Ideas, language, even the phrase
each other
doesn't make any sense.

Leaving behind ideas of rightdoing and wrongdoing doesn't mean that life becomes a hedonistic free-for-all.

Instead, we rediscover innocence. We become like children again. We return to the Garden of Paradise, to a time before the knowledge of good and evil. We are simple, straightforward, and unselfconscious. We are at play in the world. We find joy in each action. We are completely fulfilled with what is happening in this moment.

Kindness is so natural that we would not call it such. No longer do we struggle over the right thing to do, nor do we hope for any particular reward. We simply live from the heart.

When we transcend the duality of right and wrong, renouncing even the intention to be good, we fell the *asvattha* tree with the axe of wisdom. No longer does the world feel turned upside down. Our experience stabilizes. We realize the unchanging truth.

In living as a benevolent expression of truth, we discover perfect fulfillment. We experience all beings as our very self, even as this self, or sense of no-self, expands through the whole.

We awaken to radiant bliss.

Chapter VIII

ALL THAT IS SWEET

What keeps us attached to the world? It is our craving for what is sweet.

In the *Bodhisattvacharyavatara*, the sage Shantideva dispels the myth of worldly satisfaction. Shantideva was a Buddhist master who lived in India during the 8th Century. He was born a prince. Rather than assuming his father's throne, however, he became a monk at Nalanda monastery.

As do many great seers, he faced opposition from scholars who doubted and tested him. It is said that one day, while offering a teaching at their request, Shantideva rose into the air and disappeared.

These last spoken verses are known to us today as the *Bodhisattvacharyavatara*.

In this poetic treatise on the path to enlightenment, Shantideva compares indulging the senses to tasting honey from the razor's edge. There is an element of danger to worldly enjoyments. Just beneath the immediate pleasure that we so desire, is the likelihood of pain.

How interesting that what seems at first to bring pleasure has the potential to bring sorrow, as well. This is the complexity of the created world.

Still, we continue to reach out for our heart's desire, only to find that whatever symbol of wealth, power, success, or immortality we sought cannot satisfy us. Again and again, we are disappointed.

Shantideva speaks of joyous perseverence.

Having nurtured the seeds of patience in the heart, we must also develop great enthusiasm for liberation from worldly sorrows.

Shantideva advises us not to seek pleasure, reward, or accolades from our actions. Rather, he tells us to plunge into whatever we are doing, as if we were a hot and dry elephant lunging into a pool of water.

So, the mind becomes fully immersed in the present moment. This brings relief from the scorching heat of desire. We become one with the action, such that we are selfless.

In this way, whatever we are doing brings joy to ourselves and others.

The *Mundaka Upanisad,* named for those of shaven head, offers similar advice to we who struggle with desire and attachment.

In these pages, we are told of two golden birds who inhabit the same tree.

One bird is filled with desire. This bird seeks the sweetest and juiciest fruit on the branch. In its indiscriminate craving, it partakes of both the sweet and the bitter.

The other bird looks on without tasting of the tree's fruit. She leaves the bitter fruit to ripen in time and the sweet fruit for others to enjoy.

In this verse, the tree represents the body. The two birds are metaphors for the personal self and the awakened self.

We can choose to identify with either one.

The personal self seeks the fruit of action. Caught up in the cycle of pleasure and pain, loss and gain, praise and blame, and infamy and fame, we demand credit for our actions. So, we reap both the sweet and the bitter results.

Pure consciousness, however, is the steady witness. Here, we experience stillness in action.

We act from a place of selflessness. So, we allow ourselves to become an instrument of grace. We are liberated as a source of benevolence for all beings.

❖ ❖ ❖

To give up craving the sweetness of pleasure, wealth, praise, or fame sounds easier said than done. Such renunciation may seem to be more than is humanly possible.

Prayer is an act of surrender. Through prayer, we offer whatever feels like too much for us to handle to that which is greater than ourselves. Prayer helps us to connect to the infinite truth that is the source of liberation.

Prayer may be an expression of gratitude, earnest supplication, or simple conversation. Whatever words arise from the heart to connect us with the source of truth can be called prayer. The answer, too, arises as the heart's calling.

Prayer may also be formalized as the words of an inspiring saint whose path we wish to follow, or even as sacred verse.

One of the best-loved prayers for liberation in all of India is the *Maha Mrtyunjaya Mantra*.

The prayer praises Lord Siva as the three-eyed one. The third eye is the eye of omniscience, which may be marked in the center of the forehead with a *bindi*.

The *mantra* is often chanted for healing, when a loved one is sick, or for safe travels when the soul has departed from the body. Ultimately, the verse celebrates the dissolution of worldly attachment, and our liberation.

Om Tryambakam Yajamahe
Sugandhim Pushti Vardhanam
Urvarukamiva Bandhanan
Mrtyor Mukshiya Mamrtat

These lines compares the seeker to a cucumber.

The ripe cucumber falls from the vine of its own accord. There is no pulling or tugging that might damage the gourd. It is full and fragrant. It is liberated with no sign of prior attachment.

As a ripe cucumber falls effortlessly from the vine, may we be released gently from our attachments. May we be ripe and full of nectar. May it be so for all beings.

Chapter IX

BAGGAGE

The liberated sages remind us that, when riding a train, there is no need to hold onto our luggage. We set the bags down and allow the train to carry us to our destination.

Riding the train is a metaphor for living. We can trust that the train of life is taking us in the right direction. What a relief it is to give up trying to control the events and people around us, and to enjoy the ride. We simply let go of our "baggage."

We can set aside the anger, frustration, resentment, and hurt. These things only weigh us down. It's far easier to forgive than to carry around old grudges.

❖ ❖ ❖

At first, we may be afraid to forgive. After all, we don't want to be hurt again. We wear our painful experiences as a kind of protective armor. We continue to remind ourselves of past experiences, so that we can avoid similar people and situations in the future.

The difficulty with this tactic is that the mind gets stymied by the emotional charge of these situations. We remain in a state of trauma, rather than acknowledging, learning, and healing from the hurt. We may then have increasing difficulty dealing effectively with similar situations.

Forgiveness doesn't mean that we act as though a hurtful interaction never happened. We don't pretend that everything's okay, gloss over the situation, or offer ourselves as a doormat.

Instead, we find the space to engage with the person in a new way. We open to the possibility of positive transformation.

We don't judge someone according to a single interaction, a behavior pattern, or even an evolving character trait. We have faith in everyone's potential, including our own. We bow down to the soul in each being.

Of course, it helps if others are able to validate what happened, as well as the feelings that arose. When we understand each other, we find the common ground to work things out.

If comfort and reparation are not forthcoming, however, we accept this. We have the choice to patiently continue as is, or to move on.

Contemporary American theologian Reinhold Niebuhr offers us the Serenity Prayer. The opening verse may be best known through Alcoholics Anonymous. In three simple lines, it acknowledges our options and asks for guidance.

God, grant me the serenity to accept
the things I cannot change,
courage to change the things I can,
and wisdom to know the difference.

Whether we accept a situation as it is, act as a catalyst for change, or move on, to forgive simply means that we exhale and continue.

Each time we choose to let go of an old hurt and reconnect with our natural state of serenity, we empower ourselves. We relax, set the baggage down, and allow the train of life to bring us all to freedom.

Chapter X

FORGIVENESS

It's alright to make a mistake. In fact, we can expect ourselves to do so.

Eighteenth-century English poet Alexander Pope writes that to err is human and to forgive, divine.

We embody both the flesh and the spirit. We live in human form, even as we have been created in the likeness of the Lord.

This likeness doesn't refer to physicality. It speaks of our potential to share in and of the Lord's love, in this world.

To do this, we need to be honest with ourselves. We admit our failings, even as we see the truth of our divine potential. We are of both flesh and spirit.

As we acknowledge our shortcomings without judgement, so we open to forgive human error in others.

❖ ❖ ❖

Jesus Christ was a Galilean who healed the sick, raised the dead, and preached about forgiveness. Christ's words were radical for his time. He spoke of a God who is loving and forgiving, rather than wrathful.

In the Our Father Prayer, Christ offers us a teaching on forgiveness. Yes, God the Father will forgive us, but first, we need to become forgiving.

Everybody makes mistakes, including you and me. This is the beautiful vulnerability of being human.

When we forgive others, all is made right through the Lord's grace.

Christ teaches us to pray like this.

Our Father who is in heaven,
hallowed be your name.
Your kingdom come,
your will be done,
on earth as it is in heaven.
Give us this day our daily bread,

and forgive us our trespasses,
as we forgive those
who trespass against us.
Lead us not into temptation,
but deliver us from evil.

For yours is the kingdom,
the power,
and the glory.
Amen.

Through Christ's words, we ask the Father for forgiveness that is akin to our forgiving.

To forgive, we need to become willing to look up from nursing our wounds. We exchange self-pity for understanding. We set aside judgement. We stay connected to those who have hurt us by wishing them peace and healing. We open to seeing ourselves in the other. We continue the journey into light with a warm, courageous heart.

So, we find ourselves awash in spirit.

We may also seek forgiveness for all through sincere acknowledgement of our human imperfections to the Virgin Mother.

The Mother is always ready to care for the child. She brings the little one's woes to the Father that he may attend to them.

Mother of Mercy, to you do we send up our sorrows and tears.

Hail Mary, full of grace,
the Lord is with you.
Blessed are you among women,
and blessed is the fruit
of your womb, Jesus.
Holy Mary, Mother of God,
pray for us sinners,
now and at the hour of our death.
Amen.

Of course, we don't dwell on the idea that we are grieving sinners.

Confession is not about self-flagellation. The focus is not on our wrongdoings but on our continued faith and willingness to work on ourselves.

Confession is about nourishing the noble quality of humility. In being strong enough to admit that we make mistakes, we release ourselves from the painful grip of pride. We become receptive to supportive guidance.

A sure sign of maturity and spiritual progress is being able to accept responsibility for our actions.

Acknowledging our mistakes helps us to learn from them. We open to the empowering potential for change. Through awareness and sincere effort, we purify in body and mind, and awaken to divine will. So, we rediscover eternal life.

> *Glory be to the Father, and to the Son,*
> *and to the Holy Spirit.*
> *As it was in the beginning,*
> *is now and ever shall it be,*
> *world without end.*
> *Amen.*

The promise of a world without end can be realized in the heart, today. When the heart releases its long-held sorrows and resentments, we awaken to the infinite joy within.

We are reborn to live as a wellspring of grace and compassion for all.

❖ ❖ ❖

The words of St. Francis of Assisi inspire us to remember our true self, the light that lives in the heart.

St. Francis was an Italian Catholic friar who lived during the 13th Century. He is known for his love of animals, his poverty, and his piety. St. Francis founded the Franciscan Order, as well as that of the Poor Clares.

He offers these words of prayer.

Lord, make me an instrument
of your peace.
Where there is hatred, let me sow love.
Where there is injury, pardon.
Where there is doubt, faith.
Where there is despair, hope.
Where there is darkness, light.
Where there is sadness, joy.
O Divine Master,
grant that I may not so much
seek to be consoled, as to console;
to be understood, as to understand;
to be loved, as to love.

For it is in giving that we receive.
It is in pardoning that we are pardoned,
and it is in dying that we are born
to eternal life.
Amen.

Again, St. Francis points out to us that we find forgiveness in forgiving others. He reminds us to shift our concern from *How am I doing?* to *How are you doing?* We expand beyond our limited world, in which we play the central role.

Taking a real interest in those around us allows us to grow. The focus shifts from me to you. Then, we discover that we are truly able to let go of hurt and resentment, and to be free.

Forgiveness is a kind of generosity. We give people the benefit of the doubt. We stop judging others and become benevolent.

The infinite space of the heart heals all pain. We find fulfillment within, so that we can approach others without need or expectation. Instead, we are ready to forgive and to give.

So, we are liberated in the truth of boundless joy.

Chapter XI

A Tree in Winter

John the Baptist was a visionary who lived on locusts and wild honey. While he baptized with water, he heralded one who would come to baptize with spirit.

Today's Christian liturgy offers praise and supplication through the *Lamb of God*. This invocation has been handed down to us from the words of John the Baptist.

After declaring himself unworthy of loosening the Christ's sandals, John sees Jesus of Nazareth approaching the next day for baptism. John then proclaims him to be the Lamb of God.

This reference brings to mind the lambs that were sacrificed on Passover, so that the Israelites might be saved when the first-born son of the Egyptians, inlcuding that of the Pharaoh, were slain. The passing of death's hand over the houses of the Jews and their subsequent liberation from slavery are celebrated as miracles.

John's proclamation also portends the sacrifice on the cross.

When Jesus arrives in Bethabara to be baptized, John says, "Behold the Lamb of God who takes away the sins of the world."

Because Jesus Christ loved us more than we could love ourselves, he gave up his life on our behalf. The sacrificial Lamb offered himself, so that we might know eternal life.

> *Lamb of God, you take away the sins*
> *of the world. Have mercy on us.*
> *Lamb of God, you take away the sins*
> *of the world. Have mercy on us.*
> *Lamb of God, you take away the sins*
> *of the world. Grant us peace.*

Here, the sins of the world refer not only to external actions that are sparked by anger, greed, laziness, vanity, lust, envy, or gluttony, but to the internal motivation itself.

Knowing only what we have experienced since birth into materialism, most of us have been steeped in worldly desires.

The Lamb of God reveals to us a new way of living. He teaches us not to act in the hope of personal gain but to love one another, selflessly.

In so doing, we offer ourselves for the good of all beings. Body and mind are sacrificed into the purifying fire of spirit. Freed of worldly affliction, we then dwell in the peace of the contented heart.

❖ ❖ ❖

Each of us can be liberated through daily acts of self-sacrifice. We may sacrifice our limited sense of self through formal worship; sincere study, prayer, and meditation; and simple acts of kindness.

As we awaken, we begin to realize the Christ in all beings. No one is too insignificant to care for.

Oscar Wilde was a nineteenth-century Irish writer and poet. One of the most popular playwrights in London, he also wrote children's stories.

His tale *The Selfish Giant* reminds us that the Christ may even appear as a lonely and wounded child. This is the child who brings us home to Paradise.

Once was a beautiful garden, where children used to play.

The garden bloomed with flowers that looked like stars and twelve peach trees that broke into soft color with the coming of Spring.

This garden belonged to a giant who had spent seven years visiting his friend the ogre.

Upon his return, the giant shouted at the children to leave the place. This was his garden, and he would have no one else enjoy it.

The giant then built a high wall around his garden and left the children with nowhere to play.

When Spring came that year, the birds had no heart for song. The peach trees did not bloom. The giant's garden remained in the cold of Winter, for the children had gone.

Nor did the other seasons, Summer and Autumn, approach his garden. Winter's snow, wind, frost, and hail had free reign over it.

One morning, however, the giant awoke to the sound of beautiful music. It seemed that Spring had finally arrived.

Looking out through his bedroom window, the giant saw that the children had found a hole in the wall he had built and had crept back into the garden.

Everywhere, birds sang and flowers bloomed, as the children played.

One corner of the garden, however, was still covered with snow. There, the giant saw a small boy crying. He was alone and too little to climb up into the tree beside him, though the tree bent down to encourage him.

Seeing this boy, the giant's heart melted. He resolved to help the child, to take down the wall, and to let the children play again in the garden.

He opened the door to his castle and stepped out into the garden.

Seeing the giant, however, the children were frightened and fled. Only the little boy remained. His eyes were filled with tears, and he did not see the giant approaching.

The giant picked the little boy up gently and placed him in the branches of the tree. The tree's branches began to bloom with fragrant flowers. The little boy flung his arms about the giant's neck and kissed him.

Seeing the giant's kindness, the other children lost their fear.

They returned with joy to play amongst the trees and the flowers.

The giant knocked down the wall around the garden and began to play each day with the children.

Only now and again, he noticed that the little boy whom he had lifted into the tree had gone. He felt sad, asked after him, and longed to see him.

No one could say where the child had gone or why he did not return.

One day, when Winter had cloaked the garden with snow, the giant looked out of his window to see a tree that was hung with gold and silver fruits. Beneath it stood the little boy.

The giant ran to him. Seeing that the boy's hands and feet were wounded, however, he became angry.

Who would dare to hurt this child whom he so loved?

"Peace be with you," said the child, "for these are the wounds of love."

At this, the giant fell to his knees.

"You have welcomed me to play in your garden," said the child. "Today, you shall come with me to mine, which is the Garden of Paradise."

When the rest of the children returned to the garden, they found the giant lying dead, with a beautiful smile upon his face and his body covered with white blossoms.

The giant stands for our painfully inflated sense of self. The crying and wounded child is indeed the Christ.

It is the Christ who liberates us.

Christ simply means "one annointed by the Lord," or "savior." Whosoever offers us the blessed opportunity to love them is the appearance of the Christ before our very eyes.

We tend to the suffering Christ. We feed the hungry. We clothe the naked. We bring relief to the one who thirsts for the Lord's love.

At the peak of his suffering on the cross, Jesus Christ cried out, "I thirst." He then gave up the body to return to the Father.

One who thirsts and suffers like this is so close to the Father's heart. In serving each being in holy reunion, we offer ourselves to the Father, too.

When we give our lives in service, to quench the thirst for the Lord's love, we are liberated from the pain of worldly affliction.

We return to the state of grace, and to the peace of a pure and contented heart.

Believe. *Amen.*

Chapter XII

A CLAY POT

Truth does not arise from a time long ago or a land far away. It is not somewhere out there but the very essence of who we are, today.

In this very moment, we can let go of the inner tug-of-war. We can awaken to the peace within. We can be free.

Meditation may not be the only way to rediscover ourselves. It is, however, a decent path to liberation.

Like prayer, meditation is common to all traditions. It is simply sitting and looking within for the answer, for fulfillment, for the light of truth.

To meditate is like rubbing two fire sticks together, says the sage Svetasvatara in the *Svetasvatara Upanishad*. The lower stick is the body-mind, and the upper stick is the *mantra*, or the object of meditation. As we sit in silent concentration, the flame of truth bursts forth.

So, too, is truth like the oil in sesame seeds or butter in cream. The same rich potential is latent in all.

Meditation is not for a select few. It is not only for people who are calm, sinless, or particularly religious.

With sincere attention, any of us can experience a deeper sense of self.

❖ ❖ ❖

When we sit down to meditate, we let go of anything that keeps us from experiencing who we really are. We move from the outside in, relaxing body and mind, to realize our inborn state of freedom.

As we turn our attention inwards, we may become aware of long-held emotions. This is natural. We can have the courage to allow our feelings to arise, so that we can release them.

Through gentle awareness, we liberate ourselves from past conditioning, habitual response, and impulsive behavior.

The mind is a familiar companion. We recognize its reactions and its stories.

Through meditation, we attend to the mind. We learn to understand the quirks, impulses, and compulsions.

Rather than trying to shut our thoughts or feelings out, we can sit down and breathe with them.

Just listening is enough.

With true acceptance, the emotional mind calms down.

We might begin by noticing an emotion's effect on the body. Feelings may express themselves through the body as a change in facial expression, posture, breathing, temperature, or heartbeat.

In the mind, emotion may arise as thought, memory, or imagined scenario.

What arises is not bad or good. The arising itself is not bad or good.

We are simply attentive.

So, we learn that feelings are nothing to fear. They need not overwhelm us; we need not act on them. When we find the space to be still, the mind releases its disturbance.

We can picture ourselves as clay pot full of water. The pot is the body, and the water is the mind.

Now, imagine that the pot, and the water within it, are being carried along a bumpy and dusty road. As the pot jounces, the water splashes about.

This is like our everyday life, as we run hither and thither on the path to fulfillment.

When the pot is finally set down, the water within it continues to splash back and forth.

Setting down the pot is like finding our quiet seat.

Now, the pot is still. The water it holds, however, may appear to be even more agitated than it had been while the pot was in motion.

Sometimes, this is our experience when we begin to meditate.

We are habituated to the sensory stimulation and activity of the external world. When we sit quietly, the agitations of mind may become more apparent, for there is no external distraction.

Don't worry. Just as the splish-splashing water in a still pot becomes still, so the mind calms down as the body rests quietly.

In time, we experience the space of inner silence and expansive awareness. We return to our natural state of clarity.

Chapter XIII

CONTEMPLATION

When we sit down to meditate, the mind may say, *I can't stop thinking*. Regular meditators experience this kind of agitation or resistance in the same way that beginners do.

Really, there is no difference between the two. To truly discover ourselves, we must be beginners. We let go of all that we think we know, so that we can experience not knowing— *don't know mind*.

In this way, we give up the sense of personal self and expand through boundless existence.

Who am I?

Certainly, I am not the mind with its reactive thoughts and emotions. It is not I but the mind that cannot stop thinking.

Who am I?

Not this body.

Not this mind.

When we follow the I back to its source, we realize freedom.

❖ ❖ ❖

On the road to realization, we let go of all mental conditioning.

The condition of the mind reflects our lifestyle. Those of us who live in big cities and work long hours are habituated to a great deal of stimulation. The senses are continuously bombarded.

What's more, we are flooded with interaction, from the jolting of strangers, to the demands of supervisors, to the needs of loved ones.

Meanwhile, we are told through advertisements and lavish window displays that we aren't enough as we are. We need more.

Even as we are being surprised and jangled, we are expected to stay cool, do the right thing, and generally appear to be infallible. The mind works overtime to process everything that happens in an "ordinary" day.

Were we to retreat to the forest or the mountains, we would still have to deal with the mind. We cannot hide from a lifetime of mental impressions. Wherever we go, we take our thinking patterns with us.

Meditation opens us to living at ease with life as it is. Common to any tradition, meditation is simple. It is about being present.

Meditation may not change our external circumstances, but it can transform the way that we relate to them. It purifies the mind.

Meditation allows us to experience ourselves as something beyond the desires, emotions, and stubbornness of mind. It is a way to discover true love, healing, and expansion—within. It is peaceful union with all being.

❖ ❖ ❖

Here's a radical suggestion: Allow time each day to be still and think things over.

Before meditating, we can sit and contemplate. We can relax the rigidity of a tight schedule. We can open to our thoughts and feelings. It makes good sense.

Meditation is not about negating our experiences in the world. Meditation accepts what is and stabilizes the mind.

To stabilize the mind, we first need to pay attention. We attend to the mind just as we would to a child who is tired and upset.

If you've ever put a child to bed without comforting or listening to what is bothering her first, you may have experienced that child hopping up out of bed, again and again.

Similarly, the mind that has not been attended to repeatedly wanders off from the meditation seat.

It's interesting to notice that the mind processes experience even while we sleep. This is the stuff that dreams are made of. Latent desires and emotions are released from the unconscious mind through symbolic images and surreal happenings that defy logic.

It's quite natural, then, that thoughts and feelings arise to be understood when we sit down to meditate.

Processing the days events is the first step to letting them go.

What went well?

What could have been handled differently, and how can we learn from this?

Is there an unresolved situation that needs attention?

The intention behind daily contemplation is to relax the mind for meditation. We don't get lost in thought or daydream. We quietly think over the day.

How aware are we of what really matters to us?

Are we living honestly, according to our beliefs?

What simple shifts might improve our experience?

Perhaps we enjoy a cup of tea or journal, as we sit. Remember, however, that we aren't sitting down to work on any kind of project or to resolve all of our problems.

Contemplation is about spending gentle time with the mind. As is true for any relationship, the relationship with the mind benefits from regular quality time. So, trust and connection deepen. Contemplation is about being our own good parent, best friend, attentive partner, or benevolent master.

We may even have the experience when asked to sit and contemplate that we go straight into meditation. Somehow, the permission to think allows the mind to relax. Try it, and see!

Chapter XIV

MAMA

Meditation is about connection—a connection to joy, a connection to fulfillment, and a connection to inner peace.

The connection made is really to our true self. We rediscover who we are by letting go of what we are not. We let go of the enchantment of the world around us. We stop trying to acquire newer, better, or more things. We let go of who we think we are, who we want to be, and who we have been told that we need to be.

It's like an exercise in trust. If we let go of our possessions and constructed identity, what will be there? We look within to connect to truth.

We might connect through effort or through receptivity. The two balance each other, like the wings of a bird. We need both effort and receptivity in our lives, so that we can soar.

Most of us spend a good part of the day making effort. We exercise self-control to refrain from causing harm. We push ourselves a bit to offer acts of kindness to those we don't know, and sometimes to those we know all too well. We try to remain mindful in the moment.

Meanwhile, receptivity is about giving our individual actions over to the greatest good for all. We surrender control. We offer each deed, like a rose petal that floats away on the stream of life. So, we become selfless, receptive to the whole, of which we are a part.

If we live sincerely, the mind is easeful when we sit down to meditate. We aren't distracted by secrets, regrets, or worries. What we think, what we say, and what we do are aligned—with inner truth.

To live like this, in harmony with truth, is like placing the cushion for the day's meditation.

If we have prepared ourselves for meditation through pure living, then the sitting is effortless. We can simply be receptive on the cushion.

There is nothing more that needs to be done.

❖ ❖ ❖

We tend to make some effort to connect with people for business and social activities. When we meditate, however, we find the inner connection through receptivity.

We recognize receptivity in that it is not effort. Try this simple exercise.

Sit quietly. Allow the palms of the hands to rest comfortably on the legs. Bring gentle attention to the connection between the palms of the hands and the legs.

First, try to increase the sense of connection by pressing the palms down against the legs. This takes effort. You may notice that your forearms, shoulders, or even the whole body is tensing up. Perhaps your breathing changes, too.

Now, let go. Relax the arms and legs. Release. Allow the breath to return to its natural rhythm.

This time, see what it feels like to connect through receptivity. Here, connection is made through non-doing.

Allow the palms of the hands to be soft.

Let the legs to come to the hands. Feel the pleasant energetic connection that is deeper than physical touch. Let it move through to the core of your being.

When we trust enough to be open, we connect effortlessly. This is a union not only of body and mind, but also of spirit.

❖ ❖ ❖

We become receptive when we feel safe. Allow the space you are in to be safe. Choose to sit in a quiet place, where you will not be disturbed.

If this is not possible, then openly accept the surroundings as a part of the meditation.

Let your posture be relaxed and alert.

As you sit, notice that you are being supported. The support may come from the floor, a blanket, a cushion, a bench, a chair, or anything else, depending upon how you have chosen to sit.

In a deeper sense, we are always supported by the earth.

The earth supports us as solid ground beneath our feet. She asks no questions She passes no judgement. She simply holds us.

The earth supports us with her resources, as well. She provides the needed materials for food, clothing, and shelter. She asks for nothing in return.

Her support is unconditional, like that of a loving mother.

Open to the support that you feel in this moment. Allow yourselves to be held by the universal mother. Know that you are completely loved, just as you are.

Chapter XV

DON'T MEDITATE

Meditation is a loaded word.

Most of us think that we can't meditate. It's difficult or esoteric, beyond the capability of our distracted minds.

A monk who's been meditating since childhood might be able to do miraculous things, but an ordinary joe like us doesn't stand a chance.

So, forget about trying to meditate.

Forget about the hard floor, the erect posture, and the nagging itches.

Look within for a comfortable seat. The inner armchair may be the nurturing warmth of the heart or the deep peace of the third eye.

Cozy up. Get comfortable.

Then, check out the following simple verses on how to connect and how be free.

On different days, and at different times, you may be drawn to one verse or another.

Notice that some methods are based in breath, while others use feeling, sound, imagery, or thought as a point of release.

You may explore more than one verse during a given sitting.

You may simply sit and find peace.

However you enjoy this section of the book is up to you. There is no right or wrong way to rediscover that we have always been free within.

Lokah Samastah Sukhino Bhavantu
May all beings be joyous and free.

❖i❖

Just breathe.
Is there any simpler
suggestion than this?
There is no need
to change anything.
We are already
breathing.

Relax.
Notice what is.
Let go of effort.
When we stop doing,
we allow being.
Truth
is simple
existence.
To be as we are
is the ultimate
experience.

❖ii❖

Sit quietly.
Inhale
peace
and healing.
Allow the breath
to caress
any area
where you feel
tension
or pain.

Exhale.
Let go.
Be attentive.
Allow
complete
release.

❖iii❖

Sit quietly.
Rest awareness
gently
on the breath.
Notice the breath
at the nostrils.
Notice the rise
and fall
of the chest.
Feel the breath
deeply
in the belly.
Allow the breath
to breathe you.

Be breathed.
The inhale
and the exhale
suffuse each other.

One becomes the
other becomes
becomes one.
Merge
in the breath.

❖iv❖

Sit quietly.
Notice—
You are breathing.
Sense
the expansion
and release
of the space
between the ribs.
Experience
the gentle rise
and fall
of the diaphragm
muscle,
just beneath the ribcage.

Allow the breath
to caress you
from within.
Let its rhythm
soothe you.

Now,
let the attention
move deeper
within.
Feel the touch
of the breath
in the space
of the heart.

The breath's
touch
is gentle.
Notice
its slightest
movement.
Become one
with the breath,
in the space
of the heart.

❖ v ❖

Sit quietly.
Allow *mantra* to arise.
Mantra may be
an affirming phrase,
simple prayer,
sacred name,
or mystic word.

The *mantra* rises and falls,
like the breath,
from the heart.

Allow the *mantra*
to dissolve
back
into the source.
Merge with
the source
of all being.

❖vi❖

Sit quietly.
Notice
the breath.
Feel the breath
move
through
the body.
Let the breath
relax
the body.
Let the breath
relax
the mind.

As body
and mind
relax,
the life force,
prana,
flows freely.

Feel the subtle
sensation.
Prana heals.
Prana restores.
Melt into
prana,
into the
life force.

❖ vii ❖

Sit quietly.
Notice
a feeling arise.
Don't turn
away
from the feeling.
Don't struggle
with feeling.
Allow the feeling
to be.
Allow yourselves
to feel
safe
with the feeling.
Accept this feeling.
Be present
with this feeling.

Expand into
the space of peace
that holds all feeling.
You are peace.

❖viii❖

Sit quietly.
Notice
emotion
as it arises.
This emotion is
precious.
Let the emotion be
cradled by breath,
tenderly.
Allow the emotion
to calm down.

Let the breath cradle you,
rocking you gently
from within.
Experience
deep
inner
peace.

❖ix❖

Sit quietly.
Listen to the sounds
around you.
Listen without
judgement.
Simply
be aware.
Notice
ongoing sounds,
and sounds
that are
intermittent.
Notice close
sounds,
and sounds
that are
distant.

Listen without identifying
sources of sound.

Experience
the beautiful
natural harmony
that sounds around us.

Sound arises
from silence.
Sound returns
to silence.
Listen
to the
silence
that is ever-present
through all sound.

❖ x ❖

Sit quietly.
Attend to
the subtle
sounds of mind.
Such are thoughts.

Notice
one thought
at a time.
The thought may
be pleasant;
don't hold on.
The thought may
be painful;
don't push away.
Let each thought
arrive,
and let each thought
pass.

Thought arises
from mind stillness.
thought returns
to stillness that is
deeper than mind.
Rest in the
inner
stillness.

❖xi❖

Sit quietly.
Look into mind.
Notice how
one thought
follows another.
So is woven
the story of the mind.
Listen to the story
that your mind
tells.

Be a friend
to the mind.
Listen with interest,
openness,
and compassion.

There is no need
to be entangled
in the drama.

This is just a story.
This need not be
your story,
anymore.

Allow the story-
knots
to unravel.

Let it go.

You are free.

❖xii❖

Sit quietly.
Allow an adored
divine being
to arise in the mind.
See the divine one clearly.
Notice details
of face, form,
raiment,
and ornament.
Appreciate the magnificence.

Let yourselves become
this being.
Feel divine
benevolence
and power
radiating through you.

Allow
image
to dissolve.

Become the source
of infinite
benevolence.

❖xiii❖

Sit quietly.
Gaze into mind.
Let each thought be
like a cloud in the sky.

A cloud-thought floats
through the vast
expanse
of awareness.
Let the cloud-thought
move through
in its own way,
in its own time.
Like the sky,
awareness remains
undisturbed
by anything
passing through
awareness.

You are infinite
awareness.

Acknowledgements

Sun Bu-er's poem is reprinted, with permission, from *Women in Praise of the Sacred*, edited by Jane Hirshfield. ©1994 Harper Collins.

"The Sun Never Says" is reprinted, with permission, from *Love Poems from God,* by Daniel Ladinsky. ©2002 Penguin Putnam.

"Out Beyond Ideas of Wrongdoing and Rightdoing" is reprinted, with permission, from *The Essential Rumi*, by Coleman Barks. ©2004 Coleman Barks.

Books You May Enjoy

Mantra and the Goddess
by Swamini Sri Lalitambika Devi
ISBN 978-1-84694-313-3
Mantra Books, 2010

Grief
by Swamini Sri Lalitambika Devi
ISBN 978-0-9778633-6-5
Chintamani Books, 2013

Bhagavad Gita
by Swamini Sri Lalitambika Devi, Trans.
ISBN 978-0-9960236-6-5
Chintamnai Books, 2015

Lalitamba
Edited by Shyam Mukunda
ISSN 1930-0662 (annual)
Chintamani Books